Christn
Ancient Me
Modern F⌐.⌐..

Adrian Alker

St Marks CRC Press Sheffield

Together in Hope
Resources for
Christian Faith Today

This series of resource books is the result of a number of organisations working together to give encouragement and hope to those who seek a credible Christian faith for the twenty first century.

We hope that these books will be helpful to those individuals and groups, inside and outside the Church, who are exploring matters of faith and belief.

We are grateful to our authors and encourage others to offer their services.

For further information about the sponsoring organisations please see the back cover. If you wish to contact the editorial group,
email: **togetherinhope.editor@gmail.com**

The current convenor is Adrian Alker

Printed on recycled paper by Pickards.org.uk Sheffield S2 4BB

CHRISTMAS:
Ancient Meanings, Modern Faith

Contents

I would like to dedicate this short book to the people of St Mark's Church in Broomhill, Sheffield. There, for twenty years, I shared with them the joys of Christmas. Together we celebrated the messages of Christmas through carol services and eucharists, through the splendour of Midnight Mass, the joys of Christmas Day Communion and for me, above all, the creativity of the 5.30pm celebration of Christmas on Christmas Eve.

The privilege of ministry was underscored and highlighted by seeing the faces of all the children sat before the Christmas crib, surrounded by their families, as the service on Christmas Eve reached its conclusion. Their expectancy was matched by the love of their parents and grandparents and together as community we shared that deep sense of the Christ presence with us.

I hope that this book will confirm the significance of the ancient stories of the nativity of Christ for our world today, as we explore in mind and heart the profound meanings of Christmas for contemporary disciples.

Adrian Alker, July 2011
Vicar of St Marks Broomhill 1988 –2008
Currently Director of Mission Resourcing in the
Diocese of Ripon and Leeds

Introduction

Why write a book on Christmas for progressive Christians and progressive churches? For many thoughtful Christians, those in worshipping church communities and those on the edge of Church or those for whom church is now a distant memory, the Christmas stories in the gospels can actually be a barrier to faith. Singing angels, camel - riding kings, a moving star, a birth in a stable (and to a virgin woman at that) – all this seems to be the stuff of fairy tales. Yet of course it is just what so many people enjoy, as we sing our carols, watch our children in nativity plays and hear the story read solemnly in candlelit services.

One reason alone should encourage us to reflect upon Christmas: it is still the most important time of the Church's year in terms of the numbers of people in attendance. In tiny village churches the average congregation of fifteen or so swells to a packed church for the carol service and the midnight communion. This is the very stuff of Christmas card covers - a beautiful and ancient church, deeply snowbound with villagers walking over the fields to the midnight mass. So too in our large towns and cities, the clergy by Christmas Day will often have conducted a number of school carol services, hundreds will have come to the services and the income for the year considerably increased! No matter how tiresome it might be to sing "Away in a Manger" for the umpteenth time, no cleric or church could ever afford to ignore Christmas. New research has shown that in the year 2010 one in three people will have attended a Christmas service at a church.

Christmas is one of the major festivals across the world, an opportunity for family gatherings, serious retail therapy, cities and towns festooned with lights, and a respite from work. Some people will dread Christmas with its cost, the awkward family gathering, those Christmas carols played endlessly in shops and stores. For some, Christmas will be a lonely time with no one to share the day. But most people will find in Christmas something to value. I love Christmas, I love seeing the family gathered around the table, the rituals of listening to the Queen's Christmas message, the opening of presents and partying with friends. As a parish priest I loved seeing the faces of hundreds of children on Christmas Eve, of the mystery of the midnight mass and of the care and generosity of a church community seeking to help the homeless and the lonely at Christmas.

But Christmas has not been universally loved. The Puritan parliament banned the celebration of Christmas entirely, considering it "*a popish festival with no biblical justification*", and a time of wasteful and immoral behaviour.[1] In the USA you might find the greeting *Happy Holidays* alongside *Merry Christmas* and Santa Claus has become the dominant figure in the run up to Christmas. Groups such as the American Civil Liberties Union have initiated court cases to bar the display of images and other material referring to Christmas from public property, including schools. Controversially in 1998 Birmingham City Council promoted the Christmas period as "Winterval". Yet despite these and other notable cases of disquiet over the dominance of Christmas, the festival seems as secure as it has been since the earliest known reference to the date of the nativity as December 25, found in the Chronography of 354, an illuminated manuscript compiled in Rome.

Christianity is a uniquely incarnational faith, proclaiming the central conviction that in the human person of Jesus of Nazareth the people of Galilee experienced at first hand a definitive disclosure of God. The infancy narratives of Matthew and Luke and the prologue of John's gospel all arise out of this conviction that in Jesus, the Christ of God, we have learnt afresh and experienced anew what it means to be empowered to live our lives in the Spirit and power of the God of Jesus Christ. Therefore let's examine afresh those Christmas stories and discover their rich meanings for us today. We can rejoice that so many people turn to the Church at this time of year and there can be the opportunity to feed them with a faith that makes sense. Can we not immerse ourselves in the mystical element of religion, recognise the importance of the institution of the church in its communities at Christmas and use our intellect to fathom the depths of the Christmas message? Christmas does indeed appeal to the soul, mind and spirit.[2] This is why this book is written.

In chapter one I explore the place of myth and story within the gospels and attend to questions of truth and meaning and how this can contribute to the shaping of a progressive Christian faith. Chapter two covers some of the main themes and ideas emerging from Matthew's gospel and chapter three highlights some of the special characteristics of the Lukan narrative. In chapter four I offer a number of themes which emerge from the Christmas stories and explore how these ideas and concepts can be expressed through liturgy in the Christmas season. The book ends, as do all the books in this series, with suggestions for further reading and resources available for more study and practical use. At the end of each chapter there are some questions which may be helpful in promoting discussion if this book is being used by a group of people or as a study course.

So to begin, there are below a number of quotations about Christmas. As a group or as an individual reader you might like to consider which quotation speaks best to you as you think about the questions posed.

Notes

1. *Oliver Cromwell*. The Cromwell Association. 2001.
2. *From an article in the Church Times, December 2008, by Canon Nick Jowett.*

QUOTATIONS TO CONSIDER

*Christmas is the Disneyfication of Christianity (*Don Cupitt in The Independent, 1966)

'Bah', said Scrooge. 'Humbug!' (Charles Dickens, A Christmas Carol, 1843)

To the American People: Christmas is not a time or a season but a state of mind. To cherish peace and good will, to be plenteous in mercy, is to have the real spirit of Christmas. If we think on these things, there will be born in us a Savior and over us will shine a star sending its gleam of hope to the world." (Calvin Coolidge (1872-1933), American president. Presidential message (December 25, 1927).)

Unless we make Christmas an occasion to share our blessings, all the snow in Alaska won't make it 'white'." (Bing Crosby (1904-1977))

My idea of Christmas, whether old-fashioned or modern, is very simple: loving others. Come to think of it, why do we have to wait for Christmas to do that?" (Bob Hope, American film actor and comedian.)

See how the Christian year gets pulled out of shape if we make Easter an appendage to Christmas instead of vice versa (Tom Wright, writing when he was a Canon of Westminster Abbey).

The child wonders at the Christmas Tree:
Let him continue in the spirit of wonder
At the Feast as an event not accepted as a pretext;
So that the glittering rapture, the amazement
Of the first-remembered Christmas Tree,
So that the surprises, delight in new possessions
(Each one with its peculiar and exciting smell),
The expectation of the goose or turkey
And the expected awe on its appearance,.......
So that the reverence and the gaiety
May not be forgotten in later experience,

(T.S.Eliot The Cultivation of Christmas Trees, 1954)

QUESTIONS

1. **Which of the above quotations speaks the most to you and why?**
2. **What do you most like and dislike about Christmas?**
3. **Which Christmas carol would you ban and why?**
4. **Is Christmas harmful to our planet? Or is Christmas good for the world's peoples?**

1. The truth is in the meaning

Central to a progressive and thoughtful appreciation of the significance of Christmas is our understanding of the writings of Matthew and Luke in their infancy narratives. This chapter will examine a number of characteristics in these two gospels to help us appreciate the serious intent and the theological purposes of these ancient texts. I am assuming that post-enlightenment people no longer take the nativity stories as literal fact. It might be argued that for pre-enlightenment people religious belief was not as concerned with 'facts' as we seemed to have become in our contemporary society. Surely ancient peoples were as capable as we are at understanding the language of metaphor?

Midrash

Bishop Jack Spong reminds us of the obvious fact that the gospels come to us as Jewish books, written by Jewish authors (Luke may in fact have been a Gentile writing to a Jewish community), written in the main in the midrashic style of the Jewish sacred storyteller.[1] The midrashic principle is not concerned primarily with recording history but with meaning and understanding. The gospel writers had as their bedrock the corporate remembered history of their people, recorded in the Hebrew scriptures. Those scriptures in a variety of literary modes –myth, history, poetry, prophecy, allegory, story, song, - all recorded the dealings of Jahweh with the people of Israel. So much of the story of Jesus was therefore seen as a continuation of the initiative of God with his chosen ones. The ways of telling the Jesus story were Jewish ways, with endless parallels in the Old Testament, as we shall see. Midrash was the way in which Jewish teachers dissected the sacred stories looking for hidden meanings, seeking clues to new truths, yet to be revealed.

Lets begin with an example of such story 'retelling'. The writings of second Isaiah (40 – 66) probably formed the basis of Matthew's story of the magi. In chapter 60 of Isaiah you have the glory of the Lord shining through the dark night; camels coming from the east laden with spices and frankincense. The elements are there for Matthew's story. Not only the gospel writers but the whole flow of Christian tradition saw in the Hebrew scriptures a kind of framework for the story of Jesus. How did the wise men travel to see the baby Jesus? Why, on camels cry the children! Have they not seen this represented on endless Christmas cards? But no camels are mentioned specifically in Matthew's gospel story but we have almost subliminally taken them into the story because they are there in the background framework, as in Isaiah. The star, the magi, the gifts offered to the Christ child, arise out of those Jewish scriptures to make significant theological points about Jesus. If you read that splendid chapter 60 in the third section of the Isaiah prophecy, there is the fulfilment of the divine promise, God has come to his people, the light has arisen, teaching and salvation comes from Zion, not just for Israel but for the whole world. The new Jerusalem has arrived, the dream of God for God's world. Matthew, in proclaiming the coming of Jesus, the Christ of God for Gentiles as well as Jews, finds in Isaiah 60 a perfect backcloth for what he wants us to understand about the significance of Jesus. In 2 Kings chapter 10 we read of how the Queen of Sheba and her retinue visited wise King Solomon, travelling on camels from the east, bearing spices to honour the wisdom of the King. In this one illustration alone the real significance of the magi comes to us. Without the framework of the Hebrew stories, the account of the arrival of the kings at the birth of Jesus would make no sense.

Turning to the Lukan narrative, we see more examples of midrash, for example in Luke chapter 2, verse 12. 'You shall find the babe wrapped in swaddling clothes, in a manger". What would Christmas nativity plays be without a baby in a white cloth in a manger? (At our Christmas Eve family service in Sheffield we always tried to find a new born baby from the parish, and frequently ended up with baby boys and girls, black, Asian and white, varying in age up to about nine months!) Again we search the scriptures and lo we find in the apocryphal Wisdom of Solomon these words : "I was nursed with care in swaddling cloths, for no king has had a different beginning of existence". (Wis.7:4,5) . Jesus, believed by Luke to be the ultimate King of all the world is portrayed as coming to this world in a way reminiscent of the splendid King Solomon of Israel. And Jesus was born in a manger, translated perhaps as crib or feeding trough. Now again every child will tell you about the sheep and the ox and various other animals in the stable where Jesus was born and there they are, in millions of crib sets. But none of this appears in the gospel of Luke, only the word manger. But consider the opening verses of Isaiah chapter one where the prophet as the voice of God laments the ignorance of his own people. Isaiah says: "The ox knows its owner and the donkey its masters crib (or manger) but Israel, my own people, has no knowledge, no discernment." Luke places the One who was the ultimate revelation of the God of Israel in a manger. Here you see the God to whom this manger belonged. No longer will the people have no discernment. Again the use of midrash.

These examples of midrash follow right through the text of the Matthew and Luke narratives. The stories surrounding the birth of Jesus are not recorded biographical details but as Jack Spong says: "They are rather the rich midrashic weaving and reweaving of the sacred moments of the Jewish past around the life of Jesus of Nazareth.

> Take time to look at one of the above examples of how Matthew or Luke use the Hebrew scriptures to frame their story of the birth of Jesus

Parable

In their book 'The First Christmas', Marcus Borg and Dominic Crossan prefer to use the terms *parables* and *overtures* to describe the nativity stories in the gospels. As with the many parables told by Jesus, we are dealing with a narrative, a story. The language is metaphorical. The truth of the story lies in its meaning. Furthermore argue Borg and Crossan (and this is typical of Borg's analysis of the person of Jesus) the birth stories are, like many of Jesus' parables, subversive. As Jesus told subversive stories about God, so did his followers about Jesus. For example, take a title like 'The King of the Jews'. In Matthew's birth narrative the magi ask Herod 'Where is the child who is born to be king of the Jews'? It is Herod who is king of the Jewish homeland but Matthew's narrative tells us that Herod was more like Pharoah, the lord of Egypt, the lord of bondage and brutality. Rather Jesus is the true King of Israel. So too Jesus is Son of God (not Caesar), Jesus is the Light of the World, (not the emperor, son of Apollo the god of light). These birth stories subvert the dominant thinking of that contemporary world (and can challenge us too!).

Furthermore when Borg and Crossan look in detail at the two narratives in Matthew and Luke, they see the narratives as two distinct *parabolic overtures*. This leads us to read the birth stories in Matthew and Luke as having an overarching theme or deeper coherent message. In Matthew Jesus is prefigured as the new Moses and Herod then as Pharaoh. If we read Exodus chapter 1 and 2 and then Matthew 1 and 2 the parallels are obvious. The birth of Moses prepares for his great ministry as the lawgiver. So too in Matthew these opening chapters prepare the way for the Sermon on the Mount in Matthew 5 – 7.

In Luke's gospel there seems to be three important themes in this overture : an emphasis on women, the marginalised and the Holy Spirit. Mother Mary is central and Elisabeth too has her part to play as does the prophet Anna towards the end of the narrative. Luke's gospel balances male and female more than any other gospel. Secondly, Luke has a concern for the marginalised. It is lowly shepherds who hear the good news from the angels; the parallel birth is with the Baptiser, that great advocate for the poor who so influenced Jesus. Thirdly, Luke puts great store on the power of the Holy Spirit, overshadowing Mary, filling Elizabeth and Zechariah and revealing the Lord's Messiah to old Simeon. Again here is an overture to the rest of the gospel, with its repeated emphasis on the Holy Spirit fuelling the life of Jesus – at his baptism, in the wilderness, in the synagogue at Nazareth.

This way of seeing the birth stories as parabolic overtures allows us to grasp, in them, the gospel in miniature. Through these overtures Luke and Matthew are offering their readers key ways of understanding the central significance of Jesus.

> **How might it help to call the birth stories "parabolic overtures?"**

Song

Where would Christmas be without carols? Whilst many carols retell the Christmas story, adding 'extra' details such as the animals in the stable, three ships arriving, making Joseph an old man and so forth, many carols weave other material from place and time into the Christmas story. 'Past three o'clock' envisages a London night watchman, whilst 'Here we Come A Wassailing' has in mind those bands of beggars and orphans who used to dance their way through the snowy streets of England, offering to sing good cheer and to tell good fortune if the householder would give them a drink from his wassail bowl or a penny or a pork pie!

St Luke's gospel has a number of songs in its infancy narrative. The most famous is the response of Mary to the angel in verses 46 to 55, which became the canticle 'Magnificat' said or sung at evening prayer. Later in the chapter the song of Zechariah rejoicing at the birth of his son John the Baptist became the canticle 'Benedictus' at morning prayer. The Gloria of the angels was taken up in Christian liturgy and the words of Simeon in the temple, 'Lord lettest thou thy servant depart in peace', (Nunc Dimittis), have echoed from the stones of ancient churches and cathedrals for centuries.

In these songs both in the context of the gospels and in subsequent use, words and phrases, sentiments and theologies have been sung and chanted, conveying layer upon layer of meaning, often far removed from the story of Jesus' birth. The Magnificat has become a stirring hymn of liberation, the aspirations of those who seek a world where the poor are lifted high and the rich sent empty away.

Today the birth stories of Jesus form a backcloth, as did those Old Testament stories, for those who in prose and in verse see in these stories parables, metaphors, pointers to more contemporary situations where the God of Jesus Christ is at work. One sees this particularly in the songs from the Iona community, the writings of John Bell, the collects and poetry of Janet Morley. For example, take this poem from Kathy Galloway,

> *Sometimes I cry when I think of the child*
> *Born in a stable, no room anywhere,*
>
> *Growing to live in a world cold with grief and shame,*
> *Dying in agony, nailed there by fear.*
>
> *Sometimes I pray when I think of the child,*
> *Born to be human in weakness and care,*
> *Growing to stand with the poor and the prisoner,*
> *Dying to raise them in freedom to share.*[2]

The Christmas stories with their rich imagery, their symbolic and parabolic content have been a source of inspiration for artists, musicians, poets and singers over the centuries. We shall further explore this wealth of imagery in chapter 4 in its relationship to contemporary liturgy.

Parable, midrash, song – some of the features of the writings which tell of the birth of Jesus. The questions and suggestions below might serve to deepen and extend the thoughts of this chapter on the meaning of Christmas through the skills of the storyteller.

Notes

1. For much of this section I am indebted to Jack Spong's books, *Liberating the Gospels* (1966) and *Born of a Woman* (1992)
2. Found in *Hay and Stardust*, Ruth Burgess, Wild Goose publications (2005)

QUESTIONS/FURTHER REFLECTION

1. The coming of the wise men : in using passages from Isaiah 60 and 2 Kings 10 what does Matthew want us to understand about the significance of Jesus? How might we use the story of the magi in relation to Christianity in the 21st century?

2. Reflect upon the slaughter of the Jewish males by Pharaoh and the slaughter by Herod. Consider how Moses and Jesus were predestined to survive, in order to 'save' their people. What other parallels are there in the story of Moses and Jesus?

3. What does it mean to say that Jesus is the 'Light of the World'?

4. Choose a carol or Christmas song and discuss its themes and relevance for today

2. Matthew's Good News

Matthew, chapters 1 and 2

Matthew's gospel is the most Jewish of all the gospel writings. This Jewish scribe who had become a Christian was intent on convincing those orthodox Jewish minds, so hostile to the emergence of Jewish Christians inside the structures of Judaism, that Jesus was indeed the fulfilment of Jewish messianic expectations. By about the year 90 Jewish Christians were being expelled from the synagogues and Matthew may well have been a member of such a group. He wanted his fellow Christians to remember their Jewish origins and his fellow Jews to understand how he saw the significance of the Jewish Jesus. This background to the author and his writing is crucial as we approach the Christmas story in Matthew.

For Matthew, Jesus needed to be portrayed as every inch the son of David but also the son of Abraham, through whom all the nations of the earth were to be blessed. That son of Abraham message was reinforced by the visit of the magi. Just as in the Old Testament there is that oft quoted vision of the nations of the world streaming to Zion, so here visitors from afar come to the Christ child. So much of the Hebrew past is woven into the Matthew infancy narrative. Just as the patriarch Joseph took his family to Egypt to escape starvation and thus preserved God's promise to Abraham for the continuing blessings upon the covenant people, so Joseph takes Mary and Jesus to Egypt to escape death at the hands of Herod. In many ways Matthew portrays Jesus as the new Moses throughout his gospel. Here in the infancy overture of the gospel, the backdrop of Moses' birth and the story of Pharaoh's killing of the Jewish male babies in Egypt (Exodus 1.15ff) provide the parallel to the slaughter of the innocents by Herod in chapter two of Matthew. Later Jesus will be portrayed as the new lawgiver, this time in the Sermon on the Mount.

As was said in chapter one, the gospel uses midrash and parabolic overtures in these Christmas stories which will in fact set the scene for how Matthew sees the good news of Jesus throughout his gospel.

Consider these three aspects of Matthew's birth narrative : the opening genealogy (1.1 – 17), the birth (1.18 – 25), and Herod and the magi (chapter 2).

1. Genealogy – Who Do You Think You Are?

We seem to be more and more interested in tracing our origins, evidenced by the popularity of the television programme *Who Do You Think You Are?* with celebrities tracing their family trees. When I came home in my first Christmas vacation from Oxford, my father would have none of my newly acquired airs and graces – Who do you think you are ? - he asked!

Matthew is making it quite clear who Jesus is in his opening seventeen verses of the gospel. Whilst nobody will read this genealogy at a Christmas carol service (!), it nevertheless is a vital theological tool for Matthew.

Matthew structures the ancestry of Jesus in three time segments: Abraham to David (13 generations), David to the Babylonian exile(14 generations)and the exile to Jesus' birth (13 generations). So after about 14 generations something significant happens to the people of Israel – along comes King David, then the exile, now Jesus! Here is divine planning! Note how the genealogy guards against letting anyone think that Joseph is the biological father of Jesus (verse16) in contrast with the rest of the genealogy. Notice too that Matthew (unlike Luke) mentions four women, as well as Mary : Tamar, Rahab, Ruth and the wife of Uriah(Bathsheba). Here were Gentile women alongside Mary, and here were marital abnormalities. Even through these irregular unions, says Matthew, God controlled the lineage of Jesus.

With the genealogies, both here and in Luke, we are reminded, as twenty first century searchers, that so much of what we read is theology and not history. We have no idea of the real historical background to the family of Joseph and Mary, except that they were ordinary working Galilean folk living in occupied times. But Matthew is writing from the experience and hindsight of how this young man from Nazareth, who faced early opposition at home - who do you think you are?- became understood as the anointed one of God. From this experience of the Christ, Matthew writes his genealogy – for this Jesus has to be seen as the destined Messiah of God, the Son of David, a child of Abraham, a revelation to the gentiles and the Jews. It's there in this genealogy, the polemic between the lines.

But one more important thing needs to be said. Matthew is writing in a Roman world. The Roman emperors too made their genealogical claims. Caesar Augustus, Emperor at the time of the birth of Jesus, would claim through their Julian tribal family a millennium – old descent from the goddess Venus, daughter of

Jupiter and her human consort Anchises. Throughout the Empire in literature such as Virgils' Aeneid and in archaeology, the genealogy of the emperors descended from the gods would be taken for granted. So a Son of God, whose Kingdom was very different in purpose and understanding to Caesar's must also have a genealogy worth the name!

2. Birth – the Son of God

One of the key traditional elements in the birth story of Jesus is that a virgin woman called Mary gave birth to a child through the workings of the Holy Spirit and this news was communicated in advance to Mary (in Luke's gospel) and to Joseph (in Matthew's gospel) by an angel. Matthew continues to expressly declare to his readers that this was the birth of the Messiah, named Jesus, meaning a Saviour of his people. Matthew again searches his scriptures and finds the text in Isaiah 7.14 where the Lord gives a sign through a young woman with child, to be called Immanuel.

There is insufficient space in this book to examine the many different strands to the account of the conception and birth of Jesus. These can be followed up in the books recommended. For progressive Christianity some of the key points and key questions seem to be: Matthew and Luke both agree that Mary's pregnancy was not from Joseph but from the Spirit of God (the term Holy Spirit is a later Christian term which Matthew employs). Put this into the context of Jewish tradition, when we find in the Hebrew scriptures stories of predestined children conceived and born to barren or aged parents – like Sarah' s birthing of Isaac or Hannah's birthing of Samuel. Matthew and Luke could in part be following this tradition but why insist on making Mary a virgin? Is it simply perhaps that this exalts the birth of Jesus over others in the Jewish line of patriarchs and prophets? And when one puts this into the context of divine conception in the Roman world, there we find female and male gods engaging with humans in sexual intercourse. So again could it not be that the gospel writers wanted to exalt the divine conception of Jesus over all the others, even over Augustus himself and that Mary remained a virgin before, during and after conception, thus making her even greater than those in the contemporary Roman world? What is at stake here for Matthew (and Luke) is not so much virginity but theology – the theology of the child is what counts, not the biology of the mother.

If we ask what folk in the ancient world really understood about human –divine encounters the answer must be that we don't know

– could they think of these stories metaphorically or mythically but admit to their possible factual reality? Maybe. They certainly lived in a world where genetic understanding was a thing of the future. In all historical reality Mary was a typical young Palestinian woman who gave birth to many children (some of them named in the gospels) who may have conceived them by Joseph or indeed any other fellow. The earliest New Testament writings simply are not concerned about any 'miraculous birth'. Here in Matthew there is theology designed to exalt the person of Jesus.

Many Christians have sought in recent decades to downplay or question the notion of virgin birth. Whilst still being a tenet of Christianity and Islam and to be found in the creeds of the Church and stoutly defended in many quarters, the story of the Virgin Birth in Matthew and Luke is a stumbling block for many people. Moreover as the Christian tradition developed we know how significant became the cult of the Virgin Mary and how new doctrines arose about Mary's perpetual virginity, her immaculate conception, her assumption and so forth. For many, Mary brings a spiritual comfort and force to their lives; the worship of the Mother of God has become hugely embedded in Catholic Christian culture. Perhaps progressive Christians have to try to rescue Mary from this overlay of tradition and reassert her place as a strong but suffering mother who calls for our esteem as the mother of the One who revealed the love of God definitively to humankind.

3. The World's Reaction – Herod and the Magi

The third significant theme in Matthew's infancy narratives is about the visit of the astrologers/wise men/magi and the role of King Herod in the story. These elements seem to have been very important in the celebration of Christmas down the ages, as evinced in wall paintings and mosaics, carols and mystery plays and children dressing up of course as three 'kings'!

Matthew has Jesus born in Bethlehem, the city of David and the wise men follow the star to his place of birth. The readers and hearers of Matthew would be reflecting on the past kingdom of David, born in Bethlehem whose throne was established in Jerusalem. There will be the remembrance of how prophets like Jeremiah spoke of a future righteous Branch springing up, executing justice and righteousness in the land (Jer.33.15). Here in Matthew's story is another 'King of the Jews' the powerful Herod, who will do his best to thwart the rising up of any Messiah.

Note Matthew's use of the phrase King of the Jews in chapter two; it will be used again as Pilate questions Jesus in chapter 27 of the gospel. Who calls for our allegiance – Christ the King or the Caesars of this world?

The magi from the east recall the visit of the queen of Sheba to King Solomon in 1 Kings chapter 10. These figures in the story are not to be understood as figures of history but rather a way of weaving in the themes of gentile worship, the star device to announce the birth of a heroic Jewish figure and the involvement of Herod in the murder of Jewish male babies. Again there are allusions to Roman imperial theology, the most obvious being the star of Venus which leads the Trojan refugees westward to Italy.

In all of these ways, Matthew presents through this Christmas story an overture to the themes of his gospel overall. Jesus is the Messiah of God, descended from David, a child of Abraham, the Saviour not only of his people but the light to the gentiles. The real enemy is that of pagan imperial power and the real tragedy in Matthew's eyes is any Jewish collusion with that power.

QUESTIONS/FURTHER REFLECTIONS

1. What might the real family background of Jesus have looked like? And what might this say about who God 'chooses to dwell with?'

2. What are the negative and positive contributions to faith from the devotion to Mary? Is the Virgin birth integral to this devotion?

3. Look again and share thoughts about the significance of the gifts of the magi. What might be in Matthew's mind?

3. Luke – Good news for all

Luke, Chapters 1 and 2

The gospel of Luke is in many ways very different from that of Matthew and yet we know how inevitably the two gospel stories have been rolled into one story to give us the Christmas 'package'. But we also need to see Luke in its own distinctive way, with its own messages, its own infancy narrative overture, which reflects the whole of the two volumes of Luke –Acts.

Luke's gospel and the book of Acts is, like Matthew's gospel, concerned with the church's relationship to Judaism. The tone and thrust, however, is on a wider canvas, beyond Israel, in which Luke the historian writes of God's activity – God raising up the Baptist as prophet, God sending the Spirit upon Jesus, God raising Jesus up, God sending the Holy Spirit to inspire and strengthen the early apostles and disciples to take the gospel to the known world. This 'budding universalism' as described by Jack Spong,[1] is seen as the Christian movement moves into a more cosmopolitan and therefore gentile world. Time and again in Luke's gospel Jesus is shown to be the one who is the breaker of barriers that separate the human family. The two volumes of Luke are optimistic, the mood is often celebratory. If this fairly describes the writings of Luke, we can see how his first two chapters must then be an overture consistent and indicative of the whole two volumes.

We could begin just beyond the Lukan birth narrative, in chapter three, where Luke like Matthew writes a genealogy. This time the person of Jesus is traced back to the very beginning of human creation, to Adam himself (3.38). "Jesus is a new Adam, a new 'Son of God', the start of a new creation, the beginning of a transfigured earth".[2] Luke will return time and again to the book of Genesis, to not only remind his listeners of the stories of the beginnings of the world but to emphasise the new beginnings with the birth of Jesus.

1. Jesus and John the Baptiser

Unlike Matthew, Luke devotes half of his first chapter to the story of the parentage and birth of John the Baptist in a kind of parallel story telling. If Luke was familiar with Mark's gospel and the telling of the inauguration of Jesus' ministry through the baptism of John (Mark ch.1), then understandably he decided to introduce his narrative with the story of the origins of both John and Jesus. Zechariah and Elisabeth are patterned overtly on the Genesis description of Sarah and Abraham. Both sets of parents are 'righteous', both women are barren, both advanced in age, in both stories an angelic annunciation came to disbelieving fathers. If we continue to see how Luke uses his Hebrew scriptures we note that in the next generation in Genesis, Isaac's wife Rebekah, expecting the twins who were to be Esau and Jacob, experienced them leaping in the womb. (Genesis 25.22). When Rebekah inquired of the Lord what this movement in the womb meant she was told that the older brother would serve the younger. Now note how Elisabeth goes to see Mary - her kinswoman – and the babe in her womb leapt - to acknowledge surely the Lordship of Christ in Mary's womb? John and Jesus, kinsmen if not brothers, were to mirror in some ways Esau and Jacob.

Our Christmas liturgies and nativity plays give little space to the beautifully constructed narrative of the parallel stories of John and Jesus. The Baptist is for sure a hefty figure in our Advent liturgies but this opening chapter of Luke's gospel is also a beautifully constructed narrative, paralleling the births of John and Jesus– the stories of the annunciation to both parents, the songs of praise from Mary and Zechariah, the naming of the two children.

Why this early emphasis on the Baptist? Could it be that John's radical call to a more just society (Luke 3.4ff) bore influence on Jesus in the way which Luke exemplifies in his gospel of hope for the marginalised?

2. Women, Shepherds and the Power of the Most High

Three important themes seem to surface in the Christmas stories which will characterise much of Luke's writings : his emphasis on women, the marginalised and the Holy Spirit. We examine these in turn and here I owe much to the more detailed analysis in 'The First Christmas' by Marcus Borg.

Women

Throughout the history of religion and into the present day women have often been seen as a problem. 'Eve's legacy' permeates the Judeo-Christian tradition. The Jewish laws on purity couldn't quite cope with the bloody mess which menstruation and childbirth produced. Every morning still, there are some traditional Jewish men around the world who make the prayer which includes the line : *"Blessed are you, Hashem, King of the Universe, for not having made me a woman."* Women in some fundamentalist Islamic societies face the kind of oppression and lack of opportunities which outrage many women and men in more open and tolerant countries. The Church too continues to debate the role of women in its ministries and is facing increasing antagonism through what many see as bigoted and misogynistic attitudes.

On the other hand Luke in his gospel is much more positive in his portrayal of women. Mary and Elizabeth are central stage in the infancy narrative; both speak prophetically (Elizabeth in 1.42-45 and Mary in 1. 46-55); Elizabeth gives John his name; a saintly woman Anna also greets Jesus in the temple alongside Simeon. Remember in the gospels, only Luke names the various women who accompany him (8.1-3). This feels much more open and liberating as Luke balances male and female and accords worth to both marriage partners in these birth narratives.

The Marginalised

Ask anyone to name the most famous Gospel parable and the answer would surely be the story of the Good Samaritan. Luke portrays Jesus as the one who was not bound by the dividing lines which traditional Judaism had drawn against other religious groups, the poor and the sick, the lepers and the gentiles. At the home of a Pharisee Jesus speaks of a banquet to which are invited the poor, crippled, lame and blind (14.13)

Luke's concern for the marginalised and the oppressed is perhaps the most commonly recognized characteristic of his writings. This attention to the poor appears in Mary's song, reappears in the favour shown to the shepherds, surfaces in the preaching of the Baptist and in the public announcement by Jesus in his home synagogue.

It is not surprising therefore that in Luke it is not the wise men from the east who are led to the stable but 'shepherds living in the fields, keeping watch over their flocks by night.' Such folk would fit very well as the lowly and hungry people of Mary's hymn, the Magnificat. And it would not have escaped the listeners of Luke that King David – from Bethlehem – began his life as a shepherd boy.

The Holy Spirit

Luke employs the phrase about being filled or overcome by the Holy Spirit in a number of places in his infancy narratives : the angel tells Mary that the Holy Spirit will come upon her; Elizabeth, we are told, was filled with the Holy Spirit, as was Zechariah and Simeon.

As the Gospel unfolds we see time and again this empowering by the Holy Spirit: at the baptism of Jesus, in the wilderness and in the synagogue at Nazareth when Jesus gave his missional address (Luke 4.18). In the second volume, the book of Acts, it is the Holy Spirit which guides the early church. According to Luke, Jesus' last act was to instruct his disciples to wait for the gift of the Spirit and this they did, waiting in Jerusalem in prayer (Acts 1).

Here then in the Christmas stories are three characteristics, which will be clearly marked out in the Lukan writings. There are some other elements in Luke's infancy narrative, which also call for our attention.

3. Here we go up to Bethlehem

The opening verses of chapter two contain the very familiar story of Joseph and Mary going from their home in Nazareth to Bethlehem because of a universal registration following a decree from the Emperor Augustus. Luke has to get the holy family to Bethlehem for the birth since both gospel writers agree that the Messiah must be born in David's city, 'from David's line'. This is important theology – a Davidic Messiah coming to clean up the mess of the world but for Christians this would be in a nonviolent way.

Matthew has Jesus born in Bethlehem from the beginning of the story and only later after the return from Egypt did the family settle in Nazareth. Luke however has Mary living in Nazareth at the time of the visitation (ch1.26) so he has to get the family to Bethlehem for the birth! This journey to Bethlehem has of course become the very stuff of Christmas nativity plays. Poor little donkey carrying Mary as the holy family parade around the school hall! Yet none of the historical references hold water in the Lukan text : Caesar Augustus was never known to have ordered a census for the whole world all at once; the registration for taxation purposes occurred indeed under Quirinius but that was in 6 AD after Herod's death and Jesus was born, according to Matthew in the days of the said Herod. But was Luke trying to do more theologically than simply getting Jesus to be born in Bethlehem? In their book, The First Christmas, Marcus Borg and Dominic Crossan argue that it was important to set the birth of Jesus in the context of Empire. 'A decree was issued by the Emperor.......' The context is important for as we shall see Jesus would be regarded Lord and Saviour, his birth even more than the divine Emperor's birth would have a cosmic significance for the whole (taxable) world; and this birth in the very line of King David, from Bethlehem.

4. Lord and Saviour

When the angels sang to the shepherds they informed those humble men that a saviour had been born in the city of David, a saviour who is Christ the Lord. Matthew as we have seen employed the phrase 'King of the Jews' but in Luke we have these other two titles of Saviour and Lord. Earlier in Christian writings Paul had used the phrase "the Lord Jesus Christ" (for example 1 Cor.8.5-6) and 'Jesus is Lord' might well have been the earliest of Christian affirmations. Many theologians in recent decades have suggested the confrontational nature of such a title at the time of the Roman Empire. 'Lord' might be a term used by slaves of masters but to speak of 'the Lord' was to speak only of Caesar Augustus. The implications of this go far beyond a game of titles. The 'programme' of Jesus, empowered by the Holy Spirit of God, was to bring in nothing less than the Kingdom of God, right into a world which was the Kingdom of the Caesars. In other words to declare that Jesus is Lord is to invite the disciples of Jesus to work for a very different socio-economic and political order than what they had under the Empire.

Mary in the Magnificat rejoices in 'God my saviour' whilst the Benedictus song of Zechariah praises the God who 'raises up a mighty saviour' in the forthcoming birth of Jesus. The whole notion of 'salvation' would become central in the ongoing theological debates of the church. But here Luke in his gospel is again setting up for his listeners the contrast between the Emperor who was seen as the saviour of the whole world and Jesus. Roman imperial theology stated that Augustus 'saved' the Roman Empire from civil war and its consequences through victory at sea in 31BCE. Octavian would soon be entitled the One who is divine, the saviour of the world. Jesus as saviour would bring what kind of victory, what kind of peace?

Peace on Earth

Luke has an angel announcing to the shepherds 'good news of great joy for all the people' (2.10) and then the angelic host sing of peace on the earth. Peace comes from God, from heaven to earth. In the Benedictus, Christ Jesus, the morning sun, will 'guide our feet into the way of peace' (1.79) Throughout the gospel Jesus will call down peace on the earth (eg 19.37-38) But what is the nature of this peace? Crossan in his many writings on the subject emphasises that the Roman vision incarnated in the divine Augustus was peace through victory.[3] The Christian vision

24

incarnated in the divine Jesus was peace through justice. This is what is at stake. Will there ever be peace on earth through a non-violent and truly divine clean up of our world? As war upon war seems to be the only solution known to the world's leaders, will the Christmas vision put forth by Luke's angelic messengers ever become a reality?

In this chapter I have outlined a number of themes and subjects which are distinct to Luke and which are to be recognised as part of the theology of his writings taken as a whole: women, the marginalised, the Holy Spirit, peace, saviour and Lord. Each one of these subjects can themselves form a springboard to think about the significance of the Christmas stories and form the basis of a Christmas liturgy.

Notes

1. John Shelby Spong *Liberating the Gospels* (1996) see page 122
2. Marcus J Borg and John Dominic Crossan *The First Christmas* (2007) see page 94
3. John Dominic Crossan *God and Empire* (2007)

QUESTIONS/FURTHER REFLECTIONS

1. **What do you think was the significance of John the Baptist for a) Jesus b) Luke?**

2. **As a group, or on your own, read one of the songs in Luke's birth narratives (Benedictus, Magnificat or Nunc Dimittis). What are the important messages from the song?**

3. **Who are the marginalised today and how do Christians show God's love for them?**

4. **How helpful do you find the titles Lord and Saviour when applied to Jesus?**

5. **How do we pursue peace with justice?**

---

4. Humbug or Blessing? Emerging Themes

The authors of the gospels of Matthew and Luke were not writing to entertain, to provide good background stories for Christmas nativity plays. They were speaking out of and to their Jewish and Hellenistic world about the significance of Jesus whom they understood to be the longed-for Messiah, now the post-Easter Christ of the early Church. Their Christmas narratives served as prologues in their good news stories of the life, death and resurrection of Jesus. Their context was all-important, writing out of small beleaguered, originally Jewish, Christian communities in a hostile and oppressive pagan run Empire. We have seen how everything in their narratives, from the genealogies, to the stories of kings and shepherds had profound theological meaning. Titles such as 'Lord' and 'Saviour' didn't just appear unthinkingly, they were invested with deep meaning. Knowing the context is crucial to our understanding. Dominic Crossan has said on a number of occasions in his writings and recordings that 'if you get the Jesus of history correct you will get your Christianity correct.[1] I suspect those biblical authors would be amazed and rather downcast at the unthinking way in which so much of their birth narratives have been interpreted and used since the days of the early Church. They were offering blessings and often today the sceptic sees only humbug.

The context of our contemporary world is also vitally important for us who have received these Christmas stories as part of our Christian upbringing. How can they speak to us in this twenty-first century with its particular concerns? How does the liturgy of our churches, our worship Sunday by Sunday help us to be Christians in this present age? Will all those who attend Christmas services be sent out so inspired and uplifted by the message of Christmas that they will be strengthened to work for the kingdom of God on earth? That I hope is part of the aim of those who plan and deliver worship. In this chapter I will try to illustrate how themes from the Christmas stories in the Bible may feed us today.

1. Light in the Darkness

The symbolism of light and its many meanings is common to all religions, not least Judaism and Christianity. For most of the history of civilisation 'man-made' light consisted only of flame and for those of us living now in urban society we forget how much darkness can impact upon daily life. Many years ago on a visit to south India I remember my time living in a village some two hundred miles out of Madras. There was no electricity there and when it got dark you simply went into your hut and went to sleep, rising with the sun. If you go camping in remote countryside, trekking in a desert or even experience a power cut, light and darkness certainly make their impact!

Darkness can make us afraid; we stumble around, we hear sounds, we become scared. This is the stuff of horror films. Night is when we sleep and become unaware. Some people's personalities suffer from insufficient sunlight. Sickness and death go hand in hand with darkness and shadow. On the other hand light brings sight, understanding, comfort, awareness and so as a symbol it fills religious writings.

Light is the first creative act by God in Genesis. All else follows this primordial act. In John's gospel the light imagery is strong : 'in him was life and the life was the light of all people'. In other words in John there is this universal conviction that the coming of Jesus, his life and ongoing life with God brings hope for all the world and its peoples. Moreover there is in John's gospel the conviction that despite all the darkness in the world the light will never be overcome. In the Old Testament the psalmist speaks of the scriptures as 'a light to my path'.[2]

We see the symbolism of light used very specifically in relationship to the coming and birth of Jesus. In Matthew there is the guiding star, symbolising that the birth of Jesus means the coming of light drawing wise men to the radiance of his presence. From this, one could go on to deepen the symbolism – Jesus brings new understanding, 'enlightenment' to even the wise and learned. Herod wishes to kill Jesus, to extinguish the light. He represents forces working against the light, 'dark' forces of evil, cruelty, oppression. In Luke we have angels singing in the night sky, the 'glory' of the Lord is 'shining' around the shepherds. Remember too the songs in Luke's opening chapters. Zechariah in the 'Benedictus' speaks of the One who will 'give light to those who sit in darkness and in the shadow of death...' (Luke 1.79). Simeon later in the narrative speaks of the coming of the Christ as 'a light to lighten the Gentiles'. (Luke 2.32)

If we use this motif of light and darkness to its fullest effect and draw out a whole range of meanings, then our Christmas services can be a real blessing to the many who come. After all we come together at the darkest time of the year; the weather can be pretty foul, older people might feel more isolated; illness is more common and there is a winter ahead to endure. It is no coincidence that we mark light and hope then at this time of year. Long after Matthew and Luke wrote their Christmas stories, Pope Julius declared around the year 350 AD that December 25th should be the date to celebrate the birth of Jesus, for that was the time when the Roman winter solstice festival celebrated the "Birthday of the Unconquered Sun'. Peoples have always sought to see hope in the moving on from the shortest day and the longest night to when gradually the light increases day by day. At the darkest time of the year in the northern hemisphere it felt obviously right to hang on a pagan rite the Christian celebration of the birth of the One who was the 'Light of the World'. If Jesus had been born in the then unknown territories of Australasia things might have been very different!

And so people come to church at Christmas for all kinds of reasons. Young families come in a spirit of joy for their children's sake, when the giving of presents is a reminder of familial love. Single and lonely people may be seeking a deeper sense of friendship and belonging; those who have lost loved ones during the year may come seeking comfort and some kind of assurance in the Christian hope. This is why a symbol so central as light in the darkness can be widely used to bring out so many layers of meaning. Carols, songs and hymns make plentiful reference to light. The contrast of light and darkness when interpreted broadly has both a personal and a political nature. It is important in our Christmas liturgies to include both our personal yearnings and the needs of our world.

At Advent and Christmas this symbolism of light in the darkness is commonly seen in candlelit services and there are numerous liturgies built around the coming of light.

2. Conflict and Peace, Power and Humility

Much has been written and probably with some exaggeration about Christmas 1914 in the trenches of the First World War. Movingly some British and German soldiers ceased their fighting to exchange Christmas greetings. Christmas Day remains the only day when much of the ordinary routine of life stops, when the world seems quieter, when people focus on the love and joy of family and friends. 'Oh hush the noise, ye men of strife and hear the angels sing'. So many carols bid us to be attentive to the angels' message of peace on earth, of goodwill towards humankind. The Queen's Christmas message to the Commonwealth very often takes up the themes of peace and goodwill.

Yet clearly in Matthew and Luke there are ominous overtones. Herod is plotting to kill the bringer of peace; Luke writes of God bringing down the powerful and proud as Mary sings the Magnificat. In the season of Advent the Church employs many texts from the book of the prophet Isaiah. These passages such as Isaiah 11 1- 10 express the hope of a coming One who will bring peace with justice to the earth, symbolized by the wolf lying down with the lamb. In Isaiah 2.1-5 there is set forth the dream that nations will beat their swords into ploughshares and not learn war any more. It is the meek of earth who will find favour with God's Chosen One, those whom we have seen are marginalized. John the Baptist has urged people to prepare the 'Way of the Lord'. Our Christmas stories in the New Testament remind us of the dream of God for God's world. The Magnificat in Luke's gospel is one of the most challenging of political writings in the Bible.

Opportunities then arise for our Christmas worship to inspire people to work for a world of peace with justice.

3. Christmas Joy, Love and Goodwill

Central of course to the celebration of Christmas is the conviction that God is Love and that in Jesus we see God's love perfected. The gospel writers all portray Jesus as a human being full of compassion and love. The imagery of the Good Shepherd in John's gospel, the parable of the Good Samaritan in Luke, point to the heart of our discipleship as we seek to model our lives on Jesus Christ.

'Joy to the world, the Lord has come!' Throughout Advent the Christian community retells and relives the ancient yearning and hope for a different kind of world, often through the writings of Isaiah. As we have said above, that hope is for a world of peace and harmony, of justice, of light to those in darkness. At Christmas this is summed up in the joy of Christmas Day, in the sharing of gifts, the gathering around a table for the sharing of food. Again and again in the Old Testament we see the imagery of the heavenly banquet, a table laden with fine foods and wine, a banquet to which are drawn all the nations of the earth. So too in the parables of Jesus, the 'Kingdom of nobodies' is exalted as the poor and the lame, the stranger and the outcast all join in the Feast. This inclusive imagery points us to the very nature of our inclusive God. Christmas is that celebration of how that God, seen in Jesus, dwells amongst us, is incarnated in our shared meals, our shared celebrations.

This is why so many church communities and so many people of good will in all kinds of organisations will seek to offer hospitality to the lonely and the homeless at Christmas. Our 'family' is nothing less than all our sisters and brothers created in the image of the inclusive, loving God of Jesus Christ.

Notes

1. Quoted from an extract in 'Living the Questions', a DVD based study course.
2. Psalm 119.105

QUESTIONS/FURTHER REFLECTIONS

1. **In a group you might like to share ideas on how the themes mentioned in this chapter can be explored in worship.**

2. **If we put the Christmas story into the context of our contemporary society, what for you would be the principal messages from the biblical story for our world today?**

3. **You might like to reflect and/or share your experiences of light and darkness in your own life.**

4. **'Joy to the world, the Lord has come!' What is there to celebrate?**

5. Celebrating Christmas

This final chapter can be read as an appendix. In it I offer a few ways and ideas in which a church might celebrate Christmas. They are drawn from my own experience and offered as one small contribution to the stock of resources. At the end of the book is a list of further resources.

Light in the darkness

1. Festival of nine lessons and carols

Often carol services are 'candlelit'. In addition to the general candle lights why not place nine candles in a prominent position on the altar and light one candle after each reading of the nine lessons, to be accompanied by a simple prayer bringing out an aspect of the light in the darkness theme. The simple prayers can resonate with the concerns of the gathered community. For example prayers for:

- *enlightenment* (prayers for those who teach and learn in schools etc),
- *clarity* of mind, wisdom, (for those making difficult decisions in government etc)
- *the piercing of gloom* (for those who are bereaved or suffering sickness)
- *lighting up the path* (for those who offer counsel and advice, those searching for a way forward)
- *light exposing darkness* (for the highlighting of wrongs, the exposure of corruption)
- *the light of joy* (for the deep love and affection we share in our families)
- *the light of the gospel* (for the Church throughout the world)
- *the light in the darkness* (for those who live in fear)
- *the light of stars, of sun and moon* (for our fragile earth)

Of course you could be more radical and have the nine lessons centred on themes such as Light or Peace, instead of the usual Sin and Redemption motif. As long as you use some of the Christmas story extracts and sing familiar carols, I guarantee most people will be pleasantly surprised!

2. Following the Light

Take some examples from the Bible of how the people of God were guided by light – a star or a flame. For example the people of Israel followed a pillar of fire by night in the exodus story (Exodus 13ff); in the book of Numbers (ch.24) it is said that a 'Star shall come forth out of Jacob', illustrating how Israel became the chosen vehicle for God's revelation to the nations; the book of Revelation speaks of Christ the 'morning star'. A liturgy or playlet could be built around these extracts and the story of the star in Matthew incorporated.

Peace and Justice

1. The following prayer was introduced on the eve of this millennium :

   'Let there be respect for the earth, peace for its people, love in our lives, delight in the good, forgiveness for past wrongs and from now on a new start.' It's a great prayer, keep using it!

2. Use resources from Christian Aid and Cafod eg the posters of contemporary Bethlehem depicting the conflict between Palestinian and Israeli people, overwritten with the sentimental words from 'O Little Town'.

3. Centre the Christmas play or liturgy around Herod's palace, with its opulence and decadence. Into this setting bring the arrival of the wise men, the deceit and cruelty of Herod and the ultimate escape both of the wise men and the Holy Family. Contrast the kingship of Jesus and the lowliness of the stable with the extravagance and power of Herod.

Love, Joy and Compassion

1. At a carol service with a number of readings, in place of the usual theme of salvation and redemption from sin, why not choose a theme such as love and compassion? One could choose Old and New Testament readings which bear out the theme of familial love - Joseph's love for his family; the love of David and Jonathan; the love of Ruth and Naomi. Incorporate some of the infancy narrative which bring out the Love of Mary and Joseph, God's gift of love in Jesus and various New Testament passages on Love.

2. There are many good stories, which can be used as a play at Christmas and the nativity story can always be included through an imaginative linking. For example retell the Christmas

Carol by Dickens, a wonderful moral tale, where compassion triumphs over hard-heartedness. Following the presentation, have Scrooge's nephew at their Christmas celebration narrate the Christmas story. Be careful to make the ghosts rather more gentle and fairy-like so as not to upset little children!

Story time

Christmas is the time par excellence for stories. Theatres offer pantomimes, musicals and plays for family entertainment. Legend, myth, fairy tale and story seem to come alive at Christmas. Film distributors know this well, aiming to reach audiences in the Christmas holidays. Yet we know through such an array of popular entertainment there are foundational messages of love and forgiveness, of cruelty and danger, of hopes and dreams. Often the same film or play can appeal in different ways to young and old. This is certainly true for example in the Toy Story films, with deep messages for an adult as well as a young audience.

This applies no less of course with the birth narratives. At one level, as we have hinted, they may be conveyed through an infant's eyes in a school nativity play when the simplest and most literal of interpretations can nevertheless communicate profound experiences for both child and parental audience. The skill of a Christmas Eve all age gathering in a church is to create a total liturgical experience, which is both extravagant and prayerful, thoughtful and colourful, appealing to the minds and hearts of young and old. Such occasions need not be the obvious pattern of readings and carols, the resort to a "traditional nativity play' but rather a truly communitarian event with deep spiritual resonances for all who come. To illustrate how we undertook this at St Mark's Church in Broomhill, Sheffield for many years, here is a list of some of the main ingredients:

- A sense of theatre : encourage all who come to dress up in the theme of the occasion (Russian peasants, Persian kings, Victorians etc) or as shepherds, angels, kings for those children especially who want to stick to the nativity theme

- A sense of mystery and surprise: illuminate the church as you would a theatre with coloured spots, if room dress up the entrance area as it would be in Victorian England or medieval Italy (dependent on your chosen story)

- A sense of celebration with food and drink on offer as people enter (we actually served Russian cabbage pie when we told the story of Papa Panov and Baboushka)

- A sense of community activity before the "service' begins. For half an hour we would serve food and drink, have musical entertainment, craft activities and all in the mode of the period – for example flying carpet rides prior to the story of the three kings!
- A story from world literature, interspersed with suitable carols and then leading on to the nativity story
- A final scene where we gathered all the children around the crib for a blessing and a calming down!

Of course this was a huge undertaking, with a theme chosen by October, scripts written by November, members of the congregation 'volunteered' to act, to help with activities, with food, sets to be made, music to be chosen. The church was large enough and with enough ancillary rooms to undertake all of this. The point is that we were aiming to attract hundreds of people from the parish and offer them a sense of celebration underpinned with some very deep messages, which resonated with our contemporary world. And hundreds of people did indeed come for what was about an hour of intense communal celebration. This was the church community daring to let down its hair, to be unstuffy, to offer something more than the usual pious diet of traditional carols and Bible readings, all of which had been done to death by the time Christmas Eve had arrived. Admittedly it had the feel of going to a religious pantomime until we came to the retelling of the nativity story and the final crib blessing. It worked!

Some of our guiding stories are listed below and detailed scripts can be supplied (see the resources page).

a. Baboushka

b. Papa Panov

c. The Fourth Wise Man

d. Good King Wenceslas

e. St Francis builds the First Crib

f. A Christmas Carol – Dickens

There are so many more ways of creating important themes for the Christmas celebration. For example 'A Child is Born' taking the birth of Jesus and making parallels of the birth of children in different countries across time. This could bring out issues of poverty and wealth, life expectancy, prayers for the local hospitals etc. Another example is to tell the Christmas story through the eyes of one character eg Mary or a Shepherd. This brings out different feelings of affection, heartache, hopes and dreams.

Throughout this chapter I have been concerned to encourage progressive Christians in their churches to embrace Christmas and to communicate its important theology as described in this book. This means being dissatisfied with so much which is standard and banal and unexciting in much of our Christmas worship. Instead let us be imaginative, celebratory, unafraid to use story and legend, mystery and theatre to capture the mood of our community and to represent the truths of Christmas in a way which satisfies the hearts and the minds of so many who come.

FURTHER READING

Marcus J Borg and John Dominic Crossan, *The First Christmas* (2007)

Jack Spong, *Liberating the Gospels* (1966)

Jack Spong, *Born of a Woman* (1992)

Ruth Burgess, *Hay and Stardust* (2005) (Wild Goose Publications, the publishing arm of the Iona Community)

Nicola Slee and Rosie Miles, (2006) *Doing December Differently* (Wild Goose)

USEFUL WEBSITES

www.ionabooks.com - for a full list of the Wild Goose publications

www.christianaid.org.uk - type Christmas in the search box

www.cafod.org.uk - again type Christmas in the search box

SCRIPTS

For copies of the scripts mentioned in chapter six, contact Adrian Alker by emailing adrian.christine@googlemail.com